Canning and Pickling Eggs

by
Pamela K. Ritter

© October 2015
All Rights Reserved

Introduction

I am a single work at home mom with six kids. I run the Pam's Pride Recommendations blog for Budget Friendly Kindle Downloads for homesteaders, preppers, and do-it-yourselfers at Pamspriderecommendations.com. I do a lot of canning to make my family budget stretch as far as I can. I also have a decent garden that I expand every year or so. These are recipes my family uses regularly and enjoy so I thought I would share them with all of you along with some photos of our canning adventures.

I have also written Canning Potatoes and Recipes and Canning and Making Fruit Syrups. Check them out if you are interested in more great canning ideas and recipes for some year round canning.

Eggs

Eggs contain all the essential minerals and vitamins, except Vitamin C. The yolks are one of the few foods that naturally contain Vitamin D. The benefits of vitamin D are numerous and worthy of your time and attention to research all of the benefits.

Eggs also contain choline. Choline stimulates brain development and function and helps preserve memory. It is used to build cell membranes and has a role in producing signalling molecules in the brain. Choline is often grouped with the B vitamins.

Eggs are also good for your eyes. They contain lutein which has been shown to help prevent age-related cataracts and muscular degeneratio. Eggs contain more lutein than spinach and other green vegetables.

Nutritional Value

A single large boiled egg contains:

RDA: Recommended Daily Allowance

Vitamin A: 6% of the RDA

Vitamin B5: 7% of the RDA

Folate: 5% of the RDA

Vitamin B2: 15% of the RDA

Phosphorus: 9% of the RDA

Selenium: 22% of the RDA

Eggs also contain a good amount of Vitamin D, Vitamin E, Vitamin B6, Vitamin K, Calcium and Zinc.

There are 70 calories in an uncooked egg and 77 calories in a cooked egg.

6 grams of protein.

5 grams of healthy fats.

Eggs of a high quality protein with all of the essential amino acids in the right ratios. Proteins are the main building blocks of the human body. Proteins are used to make all sorts of tissues and molecules that serve both the structural and functional purposes in the body.

Eating enough protein can help with weight loss, lower blood pressure, make for stronger bones, and increase muscle mass.

It is essential to get enough for protein in your diet because studies show that the current recommended amounts may be too low to keep your body at optimum health.

Eggs are natures perfect food and studies show that eating up to 3 whole eggs per day is perfectly safe. Eggs from pasture raised hens or are fed Omega-3 enriched food tend to be higher in Omega-3 fatty acids. Omega-3 Fatty acids are known to reduce blood levels of triglycerides, which is a well known risk factor for heart disease.

Eggs also contain Lutien and Zeaxanthin. They are antioxidants that have major benefits for healthy eyes. Lutein and Zeaxanthin are powerful antioxidants that build up in the retina of the eye helping to prevent eye disorders like cataracts and macular degeneration.

Eggs also contain Vitamin A. Vitamin A deficiency is the most common cause of blindness in the world.

White verse Brown?

The color of an egg is not related to quality, flavor, nutrients, or cooking. Brown shelled eggs are produced by hens with red feathers and red ear lobes. Brown shelled egg layers tend to be larger and require more food causing brown eggs to cost more. White shelled eggs are produced by hens with white feathers and white ear lobes. There are many different kinds of breeds of chickens that have been bred and cross bred to give many different colors of eggs from white to pink to blue or green and even a deep deep chocolate color.

The color of the yolk is changed by the diet of the chicken. If a hen is eating yellow corn and alfalfa she will lay darker colored yolks. If she is feed barley and wheat she will have light colored yolks. White corn will cause her yolks to have almost no color at all.

Size

The size of the egg is usually determined by the breed of the chicken. The grade of the egg is determined by the size of the cell. The smaller the air cell the higher the grade. Grade AA eggs have an air cell that is no bigger than a dime. The air cell gets larger as the egg ages.

The egg white, known at the albumen, makes up about two thirds of the egg's weight. It contains half of its protein and a number of important minerals.

There are four alternating layers to the white part of the egg. There is an inner thick white, an inner thin white, and outer thick and an inner thin white layer. As the egg gets older the egg white tends to thing out. Older eggs spread out more and fresher eggs tend to stay more contained. Older eggs have clearer whites.

The yolk is the yellow part of the egg and makes up the remaining third of the weight.

A whole egg is about 3 tablespoons worth of liquid. The egg yolk is about 1 tablespoon of liquid. Older hens have been known to lay bigger eggs and younger hens have been known to produce double-yolks. The younger hens tend to not have a synchronized cycle causing them to occasionally produce a double yolk.

The yolk contains about half the protein in the egg and all the fat. The majority of the nutrients including Vitamins A, D, and E are contained in the yolk. Yolks are one of the few foods that naturally contain Vitamin D.

An egg shell contains about 17,000 pores on its surface.

Egg Production

China produces 160 billion eggs per year making them the worlds top producer. While the US produces about 65 billion eggs a year with 280 million hens.

A hen can lay about 250 eggs per year.

The average American eats about 250 eggs per year. The total annual consumption in the US is about 76.5 billion eggs in a year.

It takes a hen 24-26 hours to produce an egg with 30 minutes in between each cycle.

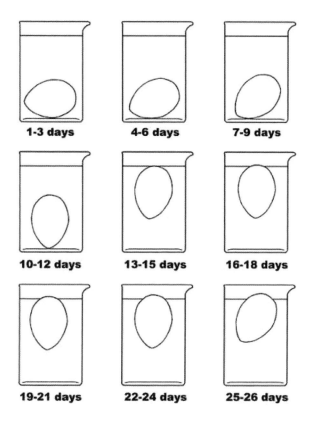

Can't remember if an egg is fresh or hard boiled? Just spin the egg. If it wobbles, it's raw. If it spins easily, it's hard boiled. A fresh egg will sink in water, a stale one will float.

How to hard boil an egg

Hard boiled and canned pickled eggs are a great and easy way to get an affordable and tasty source of protein. They are great for breakfast, lunch, and dinner or even for a snack or appetizer! So what are you waiting for?? Get boiling, pickling, and eating these tasty treats!

To get a perfect hard-boiled egg every time follow these simple steps.

If you have farm fresh eggs make a pinhole in the large end of the egg. Place the eggs in a single layer in a large saucepan and cover with cold water to an inch above the layer of eggs. Place a lid on the saucepan and bring to a boil. Remove the pan from the burner, leaving the pan covered, and let it sit for 15-18 minutes. Then immediately remove eggs with a large slotted spoon and place them in a bowl of ice water for one minute. While they are in the ice water bring a pan of hot water to a simmer. After one minute in the ice water put the eggs back in the simmering water for 10 seconds. Then back into the ice water in ten second intervals to allow the shell to expand and contract and release from the white part of the egg. Immediately roll the eggs around in your hands to crack up the shell and remove the shells under running water to make it easier.

If the eggs are older you can simply place eggs in a large saucepan. Cover them with cool water by one inch. Slowly bring the water to a boil over medium heat. When the water has reached a boil cover and remove from heat. Let it sit for 15 minutes.

Remove the eggs with a deep slotted spoon and place them in a bowl of ice water to stop the cooking. Let them sit for 5 minutes . Eggs can be peeled immediately.

Pin hole in egg shell.

Eggs in ice water after sitting in pan covered with boiling water.

Peeling Farm Fresh Egg after using the method above.

Canning Pickled Eggs

The term pickled eggs refers to eggs that are boiled to be hard-cooked, then peeled and then put in a solution of vinegar, salt, spices, and different seasonings. The pickling brine is heated to a boil and simmered for at least 5 minutes and then poured over the hard-boiled eggs in the jars.

Remember to always use the best high quality eggs that are clean and have blemish free shells. Of course eggs that are a few days old are easier to peel. The smaller the eggs the more easily the pickling flavor is able to penetrate to the egg and give you a more flavorful egg.

When storing the eggs in the refrigerator you can use a toothpick or a small knife to make a slit in the middle of the egg so the brine solution can penetrate the center of the egg to give the pickled eggs more flavor.

Peeled egg.

CAUTION: It is very important to use the upmost caution when canning and pickling eggs to ensure cleanliness and that your pickling solution is boiling to 200 degrees and that you are using hot sterile jars with sterile lids for storing eggs for more than a couple of weeks. Make sure that all utensils, pans, and work surfaces are clean as well.

Eggs should be stored in jars below 39 degrees Fahrenheit to prevent botulism.

The ph should be below 4.6.

Use eggs that are blemish and crack free that do not have splits, cracks, or tears once peeled.

If storing for longer periods of time, like longer than a couple of weeks, do NOT dilute the recipe with any water. Use only 5% acidic vinegar only.

Boil the peeled eggs to bring them back up to 200F and make sure the brine solution is at 200F before adding them to the hot sterile jars. Hot water bath to bring the eggs and brine solution in the jars back up to 200 degrees Fahrenheit.

Allow the eggs to marinate for 4-5 days before serving to absorb as much flavor as possible.

Table of Contents

Balsamic Pickled eggs

6 Balsamic Pickled Eggs

Banana Pepper Pickled Eggs

Bar Room Pickled Eggs with Sausage

Beer Pickled Eggs

Cherry Pepper Pickled Eggs

Chipotle and Adobo Pickled Eggs

Cidered Eggs

Dill Pickled Eggs

Easy Pickled Eggs

Easy Pickled Eggs with Red Beet Juice

Extra Mustardy Pickled Eggs

Garlic-Curry Pickled Eggs

Garlic Pickled Eggs I

Garlic Pickled Eggs II

Garlic Pickled Eggs III

Ginger Pickled Eggs

Ginger and Clove Pickled Eggs

Hot Chili Pepper Pickled Eggs

Hot Yellow Pepper Pickled Eggs

Jalapeno Pickled Eggs

Mustard Pickled Eggs

Pineapple Pickled Eggs

Plain Pickled Eggs

Pucker Power Pickled Eggs

Qauil Pickled Eggs

Red Beet Pickled Eggs

Red Beet Pickled Eggs II

Redneck Bar Pickled Eggs

Smoked Pickled Eggs

Southern Beet Pickled Eggs

Spicy Pickled Eggs

Sriracha Pickled Eggs

Super Hot and Spicy Pickled Eggs

Sweet Pickled Eggs

Sweet and Sour Pickled Eggs

Tarragon Pickled Eggs
Tavern Style Pickled Eggs

White Wine Pickled Eggs

Yellow Pickled Eggs

Bonus:

Banana Pepper Pickled Egg Salad

Banana Pepper Pickled Egg Appetizers

Southern Beet Pickled Deviled Eggs

The Pickled Egg Recipes!

Balsamic Pickled eggs

24 eggs hard-boiled and peeled

2 sweet onions, sliced

2 cups balsamic vinegar

4 tablespoons white sugar

20 cloves of garlic, mashed into a paste

35 peppercorns

1/2 cup beet juice

6 fresh green or red cayenne chiles, cut in half

Combine onions, balsamic vinegar, water, sugar, garlic, peppercorns, beet juice, and chiles, in a saucepan over high heat. Bring to a boil and then immediately remove from heat. Pour into the glass jar with the eggs. Seal the jar with a lid. Refrigerate 4-5 days before serving. "Slosh" around the jar occasionally to mix them up for more flavorful eggs.

6 Balsamic Pickled Eggs

6 hard-boiled peeled eggs
1/2 onion, sliced
1/2 cup balsamic vinegar
1/2 water
1 tablespoon white sugar
5 cloves garlic, crushed

Bring onion, balsamic vinegar, water, sugar, and garlic to a boil over high heat. Place eggs in glass jar. Pour the brine over the top. Seal the jar with a lid. Refrigerate 4-5 days before serving. "Slosh" around the jar occasionally to mix them up for more flavorful eggs.

Banana Pepper Pickled Eggs

18 eggs hard-boiled and peeled

80 ounce jar of pickled banana peppers

1/2 white vinegar and 1/2 water to top off the jars

Dump out the banana peppers from the jar and alternate filling 2 half gallon jars with banana peppers and hard-boiled eggs. Then top off the remainder of the jars with a 1/2 vinegar 1/2 water mixture.

Allow them to sit for 3 days. Enjoy!

You can reuse the bring and add more hard-boiled eggs to it one more time if you have brine and banana peppers left after you have ate the first batch of eggs.

Bonus recipe at the end of book!

Bar Room Pickled Eggs with Sausage

2 cups white vinegars

1 cup water

3 tablespoons pickling spices

1 teaspoon salt

1 tablespoon crushed red pepper

6 to 7 squirts of Red Hot Sauce.

1 tablespoon crushed garlic or powder

1 tablespoon dried onion.

Hard boil 18 eggs and boil 3 packages of Polish sausage until they float. Place in jar alternating until you reach the top. Be careful not to split the eggs while packing them. Combine all ingredients in saucepan and simmer for 5 minutes.

Carefully pour the hot brine over the eggs and sausage until the jar in full. Add lid and place in refrigerator to set for 3 days. Keep refrigerated. Enjoy! "Slosh" around the jar occasionally to mix them up for more flavorful eggs.

Beer Pickled Eggs

24 hard-boiled peeled eggs

1 (12 oz.) bottle beer

2 cups vinegar

1 tablespoon pickling spice

1 tablespoon parsley flakes

Place eggs in a jar. Mix beer, vinegar, pickling spice, and parsley flakes in a bowl. Pour over eggs to fill the jar ensuring that the eggs are fully submerged. Seal jar with lid. Refrigerate for 3 days. "Slosh" around the jar occasionally to mix them up for more flavorful eggs.

Cherry Pepper Pickled Eggs

12 eggs hard-boiled and peeled

1 cup white vinegar

1/2 cup pickled jalapenos, diced

1/4 teaspoon pickling salt

1 tablespoon peppercorns

1/2 cup diced onions

1 tablespoon diced cherry peppers

1/2 cup hot sauce

1 tablespoon minced garlic

Place eggs in jar with diced onion. Bring vinegar, water, jalapenos, salt, peppercorns, cherry peppers, hot sauce, and garlic to a boil in medium saucepan and then simmer for 15 minutes. Pour over eggs to fill the jar ensuring that the eggs are fully submerged. Seal jar with lid. Refrigerate for 3 days. "Slosh" around the jar occasionally to mix them up for more flavorful eggs.

Chipotle and Adobo Pickled Eggs

12 hard-boiled peeled eggs

2 cups vinegar

2 cloves garlic, crushed

1 onion, sliced

1 tablespoon salt

2 tablespoons white sugar

2 cans chipotle chilies

1 tablespoon adobo sauce from the canned Chipotle peppers

Combine the vinegar, water, garlic, onion, salt, sugar, Chipotle chilies, adobo sauce in a pan and bring to a boil. Cook until the onions are translucent, about 15 minutes. Place eggs in jar. Cover with brine solution. Seal jar with lids. Refrigerate 3 days before serving. Keep refrigerated. Enjoy! "Slosh" around the jar occasionally to mix them up for more flavorful eggs.

Cidered Eggs

12 eggs hard-boiled, peeled

1 1/2 cups pasteurized sweet apple cider or apple juice

1/2 cup vinegar

6 thin onion slices

1 1/2 teaspoons salt

1 teaspoon whole pickling spice

1 peeled garlic clove

Place eggs in a jar. Mix cider, vinegar, onion, salt, pickling spices and garlic in a saucepan and bring to a boil and simmer for 5 minutes. Pour over eggs to fill the jar ensuring that the eggs are fully submerged. Seal jar with lid. Refrigerate for 3 days. "Slosh" around the jar occasionally to mix them up for more flavorful eggs.

Dill Pickled Eggs

12 eggs hard-boiled and peeled

1 1/2 cups white vinegar

1 cup water

3/4 teaspoon dill weed

1/4 teaspoon white pepper

3 teaspoons salt

1/4 teaspoon mustard seed

1/2 teaspoon onion juice or minced onion

1/2 teaspoon minced garlic or garlic clove

Place eggs in a jar. Mix vinegar, water, dill, white pepper, onion, salt, mustard seed, and garlic in a saucepan and bring to a boil and simmer for 5 minutes. Pour over eggs to fill the jar ensuring that the eggs are fully submerged. Seal jar with lid. Refrigerate for 3 days. "Slosh" around the jar occasionally to mix them up for more flavorful eggs.

Easy Pickled Eggs

12 eggs hard-boiled and peeled

3 cups white vinegar

1 cup apple cider vinegar

1 cup water

2 tablespoons pickling salt

2 teaspoons ground mustard

2 teaspoons celery salt

1 tablespoon pickling spices

2 teaspoons garlic

1/4 onion, chopped

Place eggs in jar. Bring all other ingredients to a boil in medium saucepan and then simmer for 5 minutes. Pour over eggs to fill the jar ensuring that the eggs are fully submerged. Seal jar with lid. Refrigerate for 3 days. "Slosh" around the jar occasionally to mix them up for more flavorful eggs.

Easy Pickled Eggs with Red Beet Juice

6 eggs hard-boiled and peeled
1 cup apple cider vinegar
1 cup beet juice from canned beets
1/3 cup sugar
1/2 teaspoon salt
1/4 cup chopped onion
3 whole cloves

Place eggs in jar. Bring all other ingredients to a boil in medium saucepan and then simmer for 5 minutes. Pour over eggs to fill the jar ensuring that the eggs are fully submerged. Seal jar with lid. Refrigerate for 3 days. "Slosh" around the jar occasionally to mix them up for more flavorful eggs.

Extra Mustardy Pickled Eggs

12 hard-boiled and peeled eggs

2 cups white vinegar

2 tablespoons mustard-plain yellow prepared mustard

½ cup water

1 cup sugar

1 tablespoon salt

1 tablespoon celery seed

1 tablespoon mustard seed

6 whole cloves

1/8 teaspoon tumeric

2 onions, thinly sliced

Place eggs and onions in a jar. Bring everything else to a boil in a saucepan and mix really well. Reduce heat and simmer for 10 minutes. Pour over eggs to fill the jar ensuring that the eggs are fully submerged. Seal jar with lid. Refrigerate for 3 days. "Slosh" around the jar occasionally to mix them up for more flavorful eggs.

Garlic-Curry Pickled Eggs

12 eggs hard-boiled and peeled

1 Bermuda onion, thinly sliced

1 1/4 cup white vinegar

1 cup water

12 cloves garlic, peeled and sliced

6-8 teaspoons curry powder

1 teaspoon crushed red pepper flakes

Place eggs in jar with onion. Bring vinegar, water, sugar, garlic, curry powder and red pepper flakes to a boil in medium saucepan and then simmer for 5 minutes. Pour over eggs to fill the jar ensuring that the eggs are fully submerged. Seal jar with lid. Refrigerate for 3 days. "Slosh" around the jar occasionally to mix them up for more flavorful eggs.

Garlic Pickled Eggs I

12 eggs hard-boiled and peeled

1 sweet onion, sliced

1 cup white vinegar

1 cup water

1/4 cup white sugar

10 cloves garlic

Place eggs in jar with onion rings. Bring vinegar, water, sugar and garlic to a boil in medium saucepan and then simmer for 5 minutes. Pour over eggs to fill the jar ensuring that the eggs are fully submerged. Seal jar with lid. Refrigerate for 3 days. "Slosh" around the jar occasionally to mix them up for more flavorful eggs.

Garlic Pickled Eggs II

12 eggs hard-boiled and peeled

1 medium onion sliced

1 cup white vinegar

1 cup beet juice or water

1/2 teaspoon salt

1/4 cup white sugar

8 large fresh garlic cloves

1 pinch cayenne pepper

Place eggs in jar with onion rings. Bring vinegar, water, sugar, cayenne pepper and garlic to a boil in medium saucepan and then simmer for 5 minutes. Pour over eggs to fill the jar ensuring that the eggs are fully submerged. Seal jar with lid. Refrigerate for 3 days. "Slosh" around the jar occasionally to mix them up for more flavorful eggs.

Garlic Pickled Eggs III

12 eggs hard-boiled and peeled

1 1/2 cups white vinegar

1 1/2 cups water

10 cloves of garlic, peeled and cut into 3 pieces each

1 small red onion, sliced

1 tablespoon whole black peppercorns

Place eggs in jar with onion rings. Bring vinegar, water, peppercorns, and garlic to a boil in medium saucepan and then simmer for 5 minutes. Pour over eggs to fill the jar ensuring that the eggs are fully submerged. Seal jar with lid. Refrigerate for 3 days. "Slosh" around the jar occasionally to mix them up for more flavorful eggs.

Ginger Pickled Eggs

12 eggs hard-boiled and peeled

4 cups white vinegar

6 cloves of garlic

1 tablespoon whole white peppercorns

1 tablespoon whole allspice

2 slices of fresh ginger root

Place eggs in jar. Bring vinegar, peppercorns, allspice, garlic, and ginger to a boil in medium saucepan and then simmer for 10 minutes. Pour over eggs to fill the jar ensuring that the eggs are fully submerged. Seal jar with lid. Refrigerate for 30 days. "Slosh" around the jar occasionally to mix them up for more flavorful eggs.

Ginger and Clove Pickled Eggs

12 eggs hard-boiled and peeled

12 whole cloves

2 slices fresh ginger root

1 teaspoon black peppercorns

1 bay leaf

2 cups distilled white vinegar

1/2 cup water

Place eggs in jar. In a cheesecloth or tea ball, loosely wrap cloves, ginger root, black peppercorns and bay leaf. Place in a medium saucepan with vinegar, water, and salt and bring to a boil and simmer for 10 minutes. Discard spices. You can add some to your jar for extra flavor if you desire. Home canned allows you to make it the way you want it. Pour over eggs to fill the jar ensuring that the eggs are fully submerged. Seal jar with lid. Refrigerate for 30 days. "Slosh" around the jar occasionally to mix them up for more flavorful eggs.

Hot Chili Pepper Pickled Eggs

18 eggs hard-boiled and peeled

3 cups white vinegar

¼ cup sugar

2 tablespoon pickling spice

3 teaspoon salt

1 bay leaf

16 ounce jar hot chili peppers

Bring vinegar, sugar, pickling spice, salt, and bay leaf to boil in a medium saucepan until the sugar is dissolved. Remove from heat. Add in the juice and as many peppers from the jar of hot chili peppers as you would like. Alternate adding eggs and chili pepper mixture into half gallon jar ensuring that the eggs are fully submerged. Seal jar with lid. Refrigerate for 30 days. "Slosh" around the jar occasionally to mix them up for more flavorful eggs.

Hot Yellow Pepper Pickled Eggs

8 eggs hard-boiled and peeled

1 (12 ounce) jar of hot yellow peppers with brine

1 cup white wine vinegar

2 tablespoons pickling spice

1 tablespoon white sugar

2 teaspoons salt

1 teaspoon ground turmeric

Mix hot peppers, vinegar, pickling spice, sugar, salt, and tumeric in a bowl. Alternate adding eggs and hot pepper mixture to a jar ensuring that the eggs are fully submerged. Seal jar with lid. Refrigerate for 3 days. "Slosh" around the jar occasionally to mix them up for more flavorful eggs.

Jalapeno Pickled Eggs

36 eggs hard-boiled and peeled

4 cups white vinegar

1 onion sliced

1 tablespoon mustard seed

1 tablespoon dill seed

1 tablespoon black pepper

6 cloves of garlic

16 oz. Jar jalapenos with juice

4-6 splashes of hot sauce, or more if you like more

Place eggs in jar with onion rings. Bring vinegar, water, pepper, dill seeds, mustard, jalapenos, and garlic to a boil in medium saucepan and then simmer for 15 minutes. Pour over eggs to fill the jar ensuring that the eggs are fully submerged. Seal jar with lid. Refrigerate for 3 days. "Slosh" around the jar occasionally to mix them up for more flavorful eggs.

Mustard Pickled Eggs

6 eggs hard-boiled and peeled

½ teaspoon mustard powder

1 ½ teaspoons cornstarch

1 cup apple cider vinegar

1 teaspoon white sugar

½ teaspoon ground tumeric

1 teaspoon salt

Place eggs in jar. In medium saucepan stir together the mustard, cornstarch, sugar, tumeric, and salt. Pour in just enough apple cider vinegar to make a paste so that it is well mixed with no lumps. Then gradually stir in the rest of the cider vinegar. Bring the mixture to a boil, stirring frequently. Pour over eggs to fill the jar ensuring that the eggs are fully submerged. Seal jar with lid. Refrigerate for 3 days. "Slosh" around the jar occasionally to mix them up for more flavorful eggs.

Pineapple Pickled Eggs

12 eggs hard-boiled and peeled

1 can 12oz unsweetened pineapple juice

1 ½ cups white vinegar

2 medium onions, sliced

½ cup sugar (omit if pineapple just is already sweetened)

1 teaspoon salt

1 teaspoon whole pickling spice

Place eggs in jar with onions. Bring vinegar, pineapple juice, salt, sugar, and spices to a boil in medium saucepan and then simmer for 5 minutes. Pour over eggs to fill the jar ensuring that the eggs are fully submerged. Seal jar with lid. Refrigerate for 3 days. "Slosh" around the jar occasionally to mix them up for more flavorful eggs.

Plain Pickled Eggs

12 eggs hard-boiled and peeled

1 ½ cups distilled white vinegar

1 ½ cups water

1 tablespoon pickling spice

1 clove garlic, crushed

1 bay leaf

Place eggs in jar. Bring all other ingredients to a boil in medium saucepan and then simmer for 5 minutes. Pour over eggs to fill the jar ensuring that the eggs are fully submerged. Seal jar with lid. Refrigerate for 3 days. "Slosh" around the jar occasionally to mix them up for more flavorful eggs.

Pucker Power Pickled Eggs

24 eggs hard-boiled and peeled

2 cups water

2 cups vinegar

2 tablespoons salt

3 bay leaves

1 tablespoon garlic flakes

¼ teaspoon celery seed

¼ teaspoon peppercorns

Place eggs in jar. Bring all other ingredients to a boil in medium saucepan and then simmer for 5 minutes. Pour over eggs to fill the jar ensuring that the eggs are fully submerged. Seal jar with lid. Refrigerate for 3 days. "Slosh" around the jar occasionally to mix them up for more flavorful eggs.

Qauil Pickled Eggs

Quail eggs

½ cup white vinegar

½ cup water

1 teaspoon salt

1 teaspoon pickling spices

Small onion, sliced

Place quail eggs in a saucepan in cold water with ½ cup salt and 1 ounce vinegar per gallon of water. Boil for about 3-5 minutes. Test for doneness by breaking one egg after 3 minutes. Stir eggs while they boil a times to keep the yolk in the center. Put eggs in white vinegar for 12 hours. Then peel eggs.

Place eggs in jar. Bring all other ingredients to a boil in medium saucepan and then simmer for 5 minutes. Pour over eggs to fill the jar ensuring that the eggs are fully submerged. Seal jar with lid. Refrigerate for 3 days. "Slosh" around the jar occasionally to mix them up for more flavorful eggs.

Red Beet Pickled Eggs

24 eggs hard-boiled and peeled

2 cans small whole red beets

1/2 cup white vinegar

1/2 cup sugar

Place eggs in jar. Bring beets and juice, sugar, and vinegar, to a boil and simmer for 5 minutes. Pour over eggs to fill the jar ensuring that the eggs are fully submerged. Seal jar with lid. Refrigerate for 3 days. "Slosh" around the jar occasionally to mix them up for more flavorful eggs.

Red Beet Pickled Eggs II

.

12 eggs hard-boiled and peeled

1 can red beets slices

1 cup apple cider vinegar

3/4 cup sugar

Dash of Salt and pepper

Place eggs in jar. Bring beets and juice, sugar, vinegar, salt and pepper to a boil and simmer for 5 minutes. Pour over eggs to fill the jar ensuring that the eggs are fully submerged. Seal jar with lid. Refrigerate for 3 days. "Slosh" around the jar occasionally to mix them up for more flavorful eggs.

Redneck Bar Pickled Eggs

12 eggs hard-boiled and peeled

2 tablespoon pickling spices

1 tablespoon sugar

1 tablespoon salt

Jar of beets

2 cups white vinegar

4 jalapenos

1 teaspoon black peppercorns

Place eggs in jar. Bring vinegar, peppercorns, jalapenos, sugar, salt, beets and spices to a boil in medium saucepan and then simmer for 5 minutes. Pour over eggs to fill the jar ensuring that the eggs are fully submerged. Seal jar with lid. Refrigerate for 3 days. "Slosh" around the jar occasionally to mix them up for more flavorful eggs.

Smoked Pickled Eggs

24 eggs hard-boiled and peeled
3 cups apple cider vinegar
3 cups water
½ tablespoon worchire sauce
crushed peppercorns
½ teaspoon liquid smoke
½ teaspoon meat rub

Cold smoke on grill for two hours:
sweet red onion, sliced into 3 thick rings
5 jalapenos cut in half
1 habanero
3 cloves of garlic

Simmer cider vinegar, water, crushed peppercorn, worchire sauce, liquid smoke, meat rub, smoked onions, and smoked garlic to make a brine.
Mix and simmer brine for 10 minutes. Then add smoked jalapeno and smoke habanero. Alternating eggs and brine mixture to fill the jars ensuring that the eggs are fully submerged. Seal jar with lid. Refrigerate for 3 days. "Slosh" around the jar occasionally to mix them up for more flavorful eggs.

Southern Beet Pickled Eggs

12 eggs hard-boiled and peeled
1 cup apple cider vinegar
1 (15 ounce) can beets
1/2 cup brown sugar
1 tablespoon peppercorn
1 teaspoon salt
1 sweet onion, chopped

Place eggs, beet slices, and onions in jar. Bring beet juice, vinegar, brown sugar, salt, and peppercorns to a boil in medium saucepan and then simmer for 5 minutes. Pour over eggs to fill the jar ensuring that the eggs are fully submerged. Seal jar with lid. Refrigerate for 3 days. "Slosh" around the jar occasionally to mix them up for more flavorful eggs.

Spicy Pickled Eggs

12 eggs hard-boiled and peeled
½ cup water
1 ½ teaspoon salt
2 chili peppers
2 ½ cups vinegar
2 bay leaves
2 chili peppers
2 teaspoons sugar
2 tablespoons allspice
¼ teaspoon garlic powder

Place eggs in jar. Bring all other ingredients to a boil in medium saucepan and then simmer for 5 minutes. Pour over eggs to fill the jar ensuring that the eggs are fully submerged. Seal jar with lid. Refrigerate for 3 days. "Slosh" around the jar occasionally to mix them up for more flavorful eggs.

Sriracha Pickled Eggs

12 eggs hard-boiled and peeled
1 ½ cups vinegar
1 cup water
1 small onion, sliced
1/3 cup sriracha hot sauce
1 teaspoon sea salt

Place eggs in jar. Bring all other ingredients to a boil in medium saucepan and then simmer for 5 minutes. Pour over eggs to fill the jar ensuring that the eggs are fully submerged. Seal jar with lid. Refrigerate for 3 days. "Slosh" around the jar occasionally to mix them up for more flavorful eggs.

Super Hot and Spicy Pickled Eggs

48 eggs hard-boiled and peeled
4 cups vinegar
1 onion sliced
8 habanero peppers
7 jalapenos
½ cup pickled jalapeno peppers
2 tablespoons red pepper flakes
5 dashes of hot sauce
2 tablespoons salt
3 tablespoons mustard seeds
3 pinches of alum
4 tablespoons peppercorns
5 cloves of garlic
2 cups sliced carrots
2 cups cauliflower

Place eggs in jar. Bring all other ingredients to a boil in medium saucepan and then simmer for 15 minutes. Pour over eggs to fill the jar ensuring that the eggs are fully submerged. Seal jar with lid. Refrigerate for 3 days. "Slosh" around the jar occasionally to mix them up for more flavorful eggs.

Sweet Pickled Eggs

12 eggs hard-boiled and peeled

1 sweet onion, sliced into rings

2 cups white vinegar

2 cups water

½ cup sugar

1 teaspoon salt

1 tablespoon pickling spice

Place eggs and onion in jar. Place pickling spice in cheesecloth or a tea ball in Medium saucepan with vinegar, water, sugar, and salt. Bring to a boil and let simmer for 5 minutes. Discard spices. Pour over eggs to fill the jar ensuring that the eggs are fully submerged. Seal jar with lid. Refrigerate for 3 days. "Slosh" around the jar occasionally to mix them up for more flavorful eggs.

Sweet and Sour Pickled Eggs

12 eggs hard-boiled and peeled
1 ½ cups apple cider
½ cup cider vinegar
1 (12 oz) package of red cinnamon candy
1 tablespoon mixed pickling spice
2 tablespoons salt
1 teaspoon garlic salt

Place eggs and cinnamon hots in jar. Bring cider vinegar, apple cider, pickling spices, salt and garlic salt to a boil in medium saucepan and then simmer for 5 minutes. Pour over eggs to fill the jar ensuring that the eggs are fully submerged. Seal jar with lid. Refrigerate for 3 days. "Slosh" around the jar occasionally to mix them up for more flavorful eggs.

Tarragon Pickled Eggs

12 eggs hard-boiled and peeled
1 cup tarragon vinegar
1 cup water
2 tablespoons white sugar
1 teaspoon salt
½ teaspoon celery seed
1 clove garlic, minced
2 bay leaves

Place eggs in jar. Bring all other ingredients to a boil in medium saucepan and then simmer for 15 minutes. Pour over eggs to fill the jar ensuring that the eggs are fully submerged. Seal jar with lid. Refrigerate for 3 days. "Slosh" around the jar occasionally to mix them up for more flavorful eggs.

Tavern Style Pickled Eggs

12 eggs hard-boiled and peeled

1 tablespoon peppercorns

2 tablespoons pickling spice

4 cups vinegar

1 tablespoon sea salt

1 tablespoon crushed red pepper

Place eggs in jar. Bring vinegar, peppercorns, red peppers, sea salt, and spices to a boil in medium saucepan and then simmer for 5 minutes. Pour over eggs to fill the jar ensuring that the eggs are fully submerged. Seal jar with lid. Refrigerate for 3 days. "Slosh" around the jar occasionally to mix them up for more flavorful eggs.

White Wine Pickled Eggs

12 eggs hard-boiled and peeled

1 liter of white wine

1 tablespoon black peppercorns

1 tablespoon flaked chillies

Whole chillies

Place eggs and whole chillies in jar. Bring the white wine, peppercorns, and flaked chillies, to a boil and then simmer for 2 minutes. Pour over eggs to fill the jar ensuring that the eggs are fully submerged. Seal jar with lid. Refrigerate for 3 days. "Slosh" around the jar occasionally to mix them up for more flavorful eggs.

Yellow Pickled Eggs

12 eggs hard-boiled and peeled

1 sweet onion, thinly sliced

¾ cup water

1 cup white sugar

1 ¼ cup white vinegar

2 teaspoons salt

1 teaspoon dill weed

¼ teaspoon garlic powder

½ teaspoon mustard seed

Place eggs in jar. Bring all other ingredients to a boil in medium saucepan and then simmer for 5 minutes. Pour over eggs to fill the jar ensuring that the eggs are fully submerged. Seal jar with lid. Refrigerate for 3 days. "Slosh" around the jar occasionally to mix them up for more flavorful eggs.

Bonus:

Banana Pepper Pickled Egg Salad

Two Banana Pepper Pickled Eggs

1 tablespoon mayonnaise

salt and pepper to taste

4 peppers from jar

one or two slices of toast

In a bowl mash the two banana pepper pickled eggs with a fork. Add the mayonnaise and salt and pepper and mix well. Scoop onto a slice of toast. Add peppers on top. Top with another slice of toast for a sandwich or have it open faced.

Banana Pepper Pickled Egg Appetizers

Two Banana Pepper Pickled Eggs

1 tablespoon mayonnaise

salt and pepper to taste

peppers from jar

Ritz Crackers

In a bowl mash the two banana pepper pickled eggs with a fork. Add the mayonnaise and salt and pepper and mix well. Scoop onto crackers. Add a pepper on top of each. Enjoy!

Southern Beet Pickled Deviled Eggs

12 Southern Beet Pickled Eggs

½ cup mayonnaise

2 teaspoon dijon mustard

1 tablespoon butter

1/8 teaspoon white pepper

1/8 teaspoon Old Bay Seasoning

fresh chopped basil to garnish

Cut the 12 Southern Beets Pickled Eggs in half. Scoop out the yolks in a medium sized bowl. Use as many onions from the jar as you desire, one or two or more slices, and mince or dice them, add to bowl. Add in mayonnaise, mustard, butter, pepper, and Old Bay. Mix with a hand mixer.

Pipe mixture into the Southern Beet Pickled Egg white halves.

Garnish with chopped basil.

I hope you enjoyed this book and that you check out my website at PamsPrideRecommendations.com for more Budget Friendly Kindle downloads for homesteaders, preppers, and do-it-yourselfers. Also be sure to check out my other book Canning Potatoes and Recipes and Canning and Making Fruit Syrups.
Thank you,
Pam

© October 2015

All Rights Reserved

No part of this book may be reproduced or copied without written permission from Pamela Ritter.

Printed in Great Britain
by Amazon